TIMBUKTU

by Kathryn Harper
illustrated by Angeles Peinador

 CAMBRIDGE UNIVERSITY PRESS

 UCL Institute of Education

1. All the way to Timbuktu

My name is Musa. I'm named after Mansa Musa.
He was a great emperor from Timbuktu who lived
700 years ago. Not many people have heard
of him and they don't know where
Timbuktu is. But I know lots about
my city. Let me tell you all about it.

Timbuktu is a real city in Mali,
Africa. It's very old and isolated.
Some people think it is a mysterious
city, full of gold and riches. That was
true, hundreds of years ago. Then,
it was one of the greatest centres
of trade, learning and culture
in the world. It's a little different today.

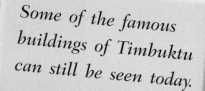

Some of the famous buildings of Timbuktu can still be seen today.

2. Where is Timbuktu?

Timbuktu is far away from other big towns and cities, but it's easy to find on a map. A writer once said:

'Timbuktu - where the camel meets the canoe.'

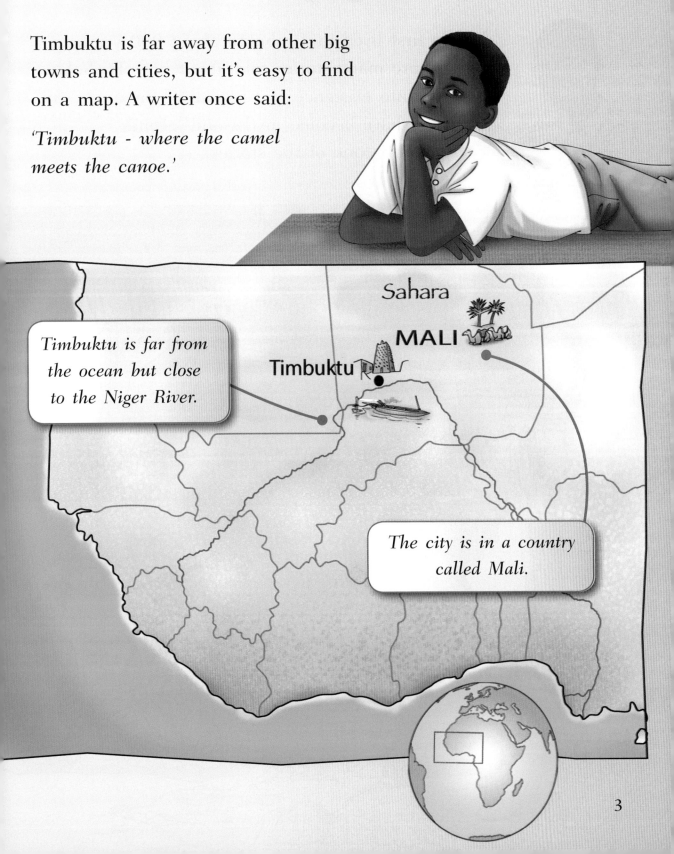

Timbuktu is far from the ocean but close to the Niger River.

Sahara

MALI

Timbuktu

The city is in a country called Mali.

3

3. The Beginning of Timbuktu

People first lived in Timbuktu about 900 years ago.
There are many stories told about how Timbuktu
came into existence and not all of them are true.
They have become myths and legends.
Here is one of the stories.

4

BUKTU'S WELLS

The Touareg people were nomads. They moved from place to place with their animals and lived in tents that they could easily put up and take down. Buktu was an old Touareg woman.

'I'm tired and I'm not travelling in the dry season,' said Buktu. 'I want to find a place to rest with my animals.'

She went to the Niger River.

'Ouch! There are too many **mosquitoes**,' she said. 'I don't want to camp here.'

She found a place with **wells** a little distance away.

'There's lots of water here,' she said. 'That's good for my animals. I'll stay here.'

She put up her tent and lived by the wells. She took good care of the animals. The water was sweet and good. Her animals were fat and happy.

Many caravans came to camp there. The caravans were long lines of animals and people travelling together. They filled up with water and rested. More and more people came to live there.

People started to trade at the camp. It grew bigger and bigger. Long after Buktu was gone, her name lived on as the camp was called Tim Buktu or the Well of Buktu.

4. Caravans

I live in a big desert and there aren't many rivers or oceans that can take us to other places. Today we have aeroplanes, but long ago, people used to travel in caravans over land. Travelling in a big group kept them safe from bandits and thieves.

There were great civilizations in many parts of West Africa. They were rich and wanted to trade with other people from places like the Middle East and North Africa.

The caravans travelled very far and the trips took a long time. This was one reason why Timbuktu became so important. With its central location, it was the perfect place for caravans to meet, rest and trade before moving on to other places. Gold, **ivory**, **ebony** and slaves from the south of Timbuktu were traded for salt and copper from the Sahara Desert.

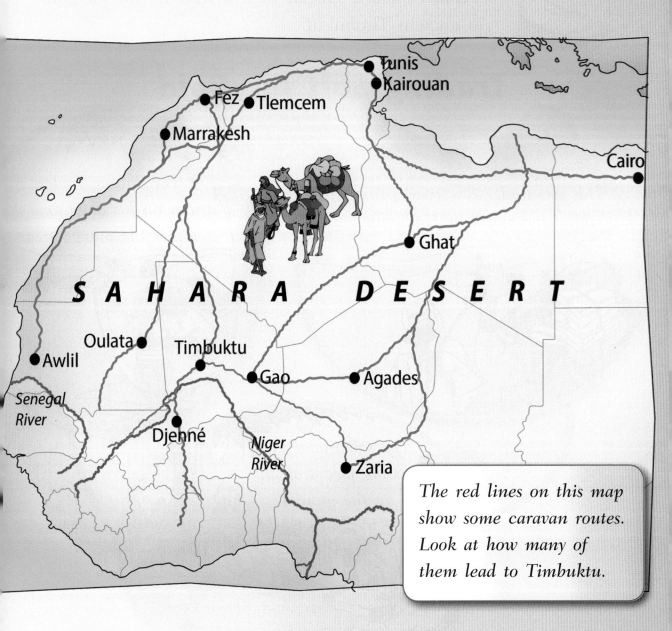

The red lines on this map show some caravan routes. Look at how many of them lead to Timbuktu.

5. Trading

Look at this piece of salt. You probably see salt every day. You eat it every day and don't think about it. But it used to be very precious. Long ago, it was worth almost as much as gold. Traders had a special way of trading salt for gold in ancient Timbuktu.

Trading Salt for Gold

1 This salt trader is a Toureg from the desert north of Timbuktu.

2 The salt trader lays his big pieces of salt on the ground.

3 The Tourag trader drums on his deba and sits under the mango tree.

The gold trader from Ghana wants to buy the salt. He puts some gold beside it and he walks away.

5 The salt trader looks at the gold. It isn't enough. He sits down under the mango tree again.

6 The gold trader puts some more gold beside the salt.

7 This time the salt trader is happy and takes the gold

8 The gold trader now has his salt.

6. Mansa Musa

When people talk about the mystery of Timbuktu, they often mean the time of my favourite emperor, Mansa Musa. He ruled Mali about 700 years ago. Some people think he was the richest man, ever. He became very famous when he travelled with a huge caravan from Timbuktu to Mecca in Saudi Arabia. That was a very long way. That means that the caravan crossed from West to East Africa and into the Arabian Peninsula. Some of the people rode horses, but many of them walked.

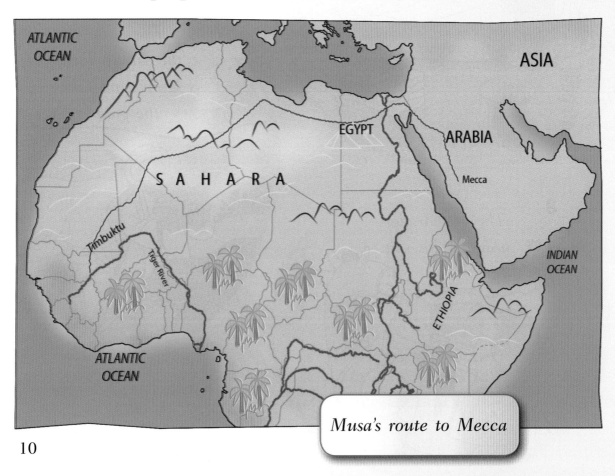

Musa's route to Mecca

Mansa Musa was Emperor of Mali about 700 years ago.

Mansa Musa's caravan was truly **legendary**. In total, about 60,000 people travelled in the caravan. There were families, traders, and servants. They dressed in fantastic clothes in bright and beautiful colours. Even the slaves dressed in silk and carried staffs decorated with gold.

There were lots of animals to help move the people, food and gifts. Each camel carried 150 kilos of gold. At night, the caravan stopped and the tents were set up and meals were prepared. After a long day travelling, people needed a good sleep.

As the caravan passed through towns and villages, people couldn't believe their eyes. The caravan was so long, so rich and so exotic. It seemed never-ending. Every so often, Mansa Musa stopped and gave gold to poor people. They must have been surprised when this great emperor stopped to give them gold!

Soon, people all over the world start talking about this emperor and his amazing caravan. They become very **curious** about his wonderful and mysterious empire in the middle of Africa.

7. Returning to Timbuktu

Mansa Musa wanted to learn from his travels and help improve his empire. When he travelled, he gave many gifts but he brought back the most important thing - knowledge. He brought back people and ideas that would change Mali and Timbuktu for hundreds of years. He helped build Timbuktu into a great city of learning and culture.

He brought people to Timbuktu who could improve the city. One person was an **architect** called Abou Ishaq es-Saheli. He was originally from Spain, but met Mansa Musa in Saudi Arabia. They say that Mansa Musa paid him 400 kilos of gold to design the Djinguereber Mosque. This is part of the University of Timbuktu. After 600 years, it is still being used today by students in my own family!

The walls of the mosque are made of fibre, straw, wood and mud.

There are three courtyards.

Djinguereber Mosque

There are 25 rows of pillars.

There are two **minarets**.

13

8. The Golden Age

200 years after Mansa Musa, Timbuktu was a very different place. The City of Gold was now in its Golden Age.

I like to imagine what it was like to walk through the streets back then. It must have been a busy, colourful place. There were golden mango trees and **canals** that brought freshness to the warm air. There were mosques, palaces, libraries, houses, tents and markets. Many of the fantastic mud buildings looked as if they had grown straight out of the earth.

There were many, many people. More than 200,000 lived in Timbuktu then. There were people from all over Africa, from Egypt, Persia, Arabia and Morocco. They wore beautiful, colourful clothes. They made a huge **din** when they bought and sold, sang and danced, laughed and argued.

9. Learning

I love learning about things and that's why I love Timbuktu. In its Golden Age, it was the greatest place of learning in the world. Everywhere you looked, there were students from many different countries. They studied many things, such as: religion, law, poetry, maths, science, medicine and astronomy.

Timbuktu became a great place for sharing knowledge and **exchanging** ideas. Teaching was a very important profession, and teachers were greatly respected and admired by their students. In many ways, the knowledge they traded was as important as the trade of gold and salt.

10. Books

Some people say that Timbuktu's greatest treasure from the Golden Age was its wonderful collection of books. That's because the information in books was so precious. Many people think that it was really books that made Timbuktu so rich in its Golden Age.

At that time, there were no printing presses, so each book was carefully written, drawn and decorated by hand – usually by students. It took a long time to make each of these beautiful books.

Wealthy families showed how important they were by the number of books they owned. Many wealthy families collected and stored books for long periods of time. These huge collections of books formed a priceless record of the world over many centuries.

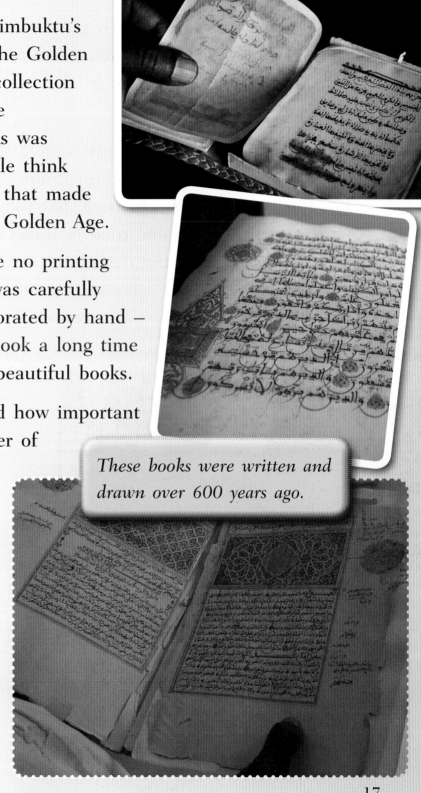

These books were written and drawn over 600 years ago.

11. European Dreams

People in Europe were extremely curious about Timbuktu and its treasures. They heard about how rich Mansa Musa and Timbuktu were. They thought that the streets were made of gold.

For hundreds of years, Europeans wanted to find Timbuktu, but it was a difficult place to visit. Some explorers took boats to the west coast of Africa, but they often died from tropical diseases. Some tried to travel over the desert, but it was too dangerous. For a long time, Timbuktu remained a mysterious place for them.

Then, in 1824, some people in France offered a big reward for the first European to reach Timbuktu and return alive. In 1828, René Caillié from France travelled to Timbuktu from West Africa with a caravan. He pretended to be Egyptian and was helped by a local family. But Timbuktu was no longer in its Golden Age. By that time, people travelled more by sea to trade, because it was quicker and easier than travelling over land. Timbuktu was no longer rich and its roads never had been gold. Caillié was disappointed. But he went back to France and became famous, telling his story all over the country.

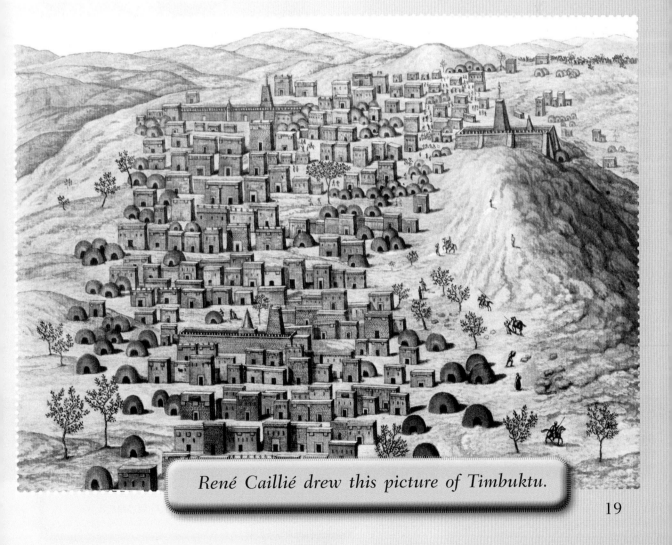

René Caillié drew this picture of Timbuktu.

12. Harder Times Now

Today, life in Timbuktu is not always easy. It is no longer a rich place and there are fewer people. **Desertification** has taken over the area and it is difficult to grow food. People often go hungry. Mango trees don't grow any more. The canals don't work and many of the beautiful buildings are no longer there.

The desert has damaged many of Timbuktu's buildings as the wind whips sand against the stones.

In 2012, there was an attack and some of Timbuktu's beautiful buildings and many very precious books were destroyed. People in Timbuktu have always loved books. A man named Abdel Kader Haidara and his friends hid thousands of books in metal boxes. They secretly took them away and hid them

Here is Abdel Kader Haidara with some of the boxes of books he saved.

to prevent them from being destroyed. They had to make many trips by mule cart, truck, boat and taxi. They managed to save over 300,000 books.

With the help of brave people like Abdel Kader Haidara, the people of Timbuktu can continue to keep knowledge for the world and some of its greatness can live on.

Glossary

architect   someone who designs buildings

canals   man-made waterways

curious   wanting to know more about something

desertification   process by which land turns into desert

din   loud noise

ebony   very dark wood

exchanging   swapping

ivory   light-coloured material made from the horns and tusks of animals, such as elephants

legendary   well-known over time

minarets   towers of a mosque

mosquitos   small insects that drink the blood of animals and people

wells   deep holes in the ground from where water can be collected

Index

TIMBUKTU *Kathryn Harper*

Teaching notes written by Sue Bodman and Glen Franklin

Using this book

Content/theme/subject

This book combines history, geography, fact and legend to explore the city of Timbuktu in Mali, Africa. The book uses a narrative voice, as the character of Musa shares his experiences with the reader, as well as a range of other appropriate genre styles. Illustrations are used alongside photographs to compare old and new Timbuktu. A conclusion is drawn about preserving the past for future generations.

Language structure

- Grammatical constructions follow the expected conventions for the genre, including first person narrative: *'I live in a big desert'*, (p.6); *'I love learning about things'* (p.16), and past tense for non-chronological report.

- The voice of the narrator serves to engage the reader: *'Let me tell you all about it'* (p.2); *'Look at this piece of salt'* (p.8).

Book structure/visual features

- Diagrams, maps and charts exemplify the points made.

- Labels, captions and fact boxes support the information in the main text.

Vocabulary and comprehension

- Topic-specific vocabulary (such as *'ebony'* and *'ivory'* on p.7) is supported through non-fiction devices in the text or defined in the glossary.

- The narrative voice supports comprehension through establishing a dialogue with the reader (see p.8, for example).

Curriculum links

Geography – Musa tells the reader that Timbuktu is a hard place to reach. Use maps to locate Timbuktu, and use the internet to explore the travel options to that country from your region.

History – Research the real historical figure of Mansa Musa. You may also wish to find out more about the salt trade, linked with other aspects of trade and commerce (such as silks and spices) relevant to your region.

Learning outcomes

Children can:

- consider how choice of layout and design relate to the intended audience

- note how sentence structure choices convey the author's intent and meaning

- use phonic/spelling knowledge, along with grammatical and contextual cues, to solve new or unfamiliar words.

Planning for guided reading

Lesson One The effects of layout and design

Give each child a copy of the book. Read the title together, demonstrating reading in syllable chunks if 'Timbuktu' is an unfamiliar word. Ask: *Has anyone heard of Timbuktu? Do you know anything about it?* Take the children to p.2 and read the first paragraph to establish that Timbuktu is an ancient city in Mali, in Africa. Consider the purpose of the book: although it is a non-fiction text, there are also aspects of story which could confuse less-experienced young readers.

Discuss why the book might be using these different design features (the narrator figure; the mix of photos and illustrations; the story format on p.5; the explanation layout on pp.8-9). Point out how the book mixes information about the present day (Chapter 13, for example) with historical details, as in Chapter 6. Turn to pp.12-13, and note how the past and present combine in this chapter.

Set an independent reading task to read up to p.15. Whilst the purpose of a non-fiction text is to find information, this book also provides a useful opportunity to consider how decision about layout and design can support the reader. Tell the children that as they read, you want them to think about the effectiveness of design choices, and how these help them understand the text. Listen in as they read, prompting as appropriate: *These pages look very different to the rest of the book* (pp.8-9). *Why do you think this part of the text is designed like this?* Discuss how this section has elements of explanation texts, seeking to explain how something happens.